DynamoDB Hot Key Troubleshooting

Table of Contents

Chapter 1. Introduction

Dive into the intricate world of DynamoDB with our Special Report: "DynamoDB Hot Key Troubleshooting." With an intense focus on hot keys and how to address issues surrounding them, we take you step-by-step through the concepts, practices, and strategies vital to avoiding and managing this common challenge in DynamoDB operations. While the topic has a technical flair, this report is grounded in practicality, catering extensively to both novices and experts, dedicated to demystifying complex aspects into simpler, digestible nuggets of knowledge. So, gear up for an enriching journey that promises to enhance your DynamoDB operational efficiency and equip you with actionable troubleshooting skills to preemptively tackle hot key-related conundrums.

Chapter 2. Understanding DynamoDB and Hot Keys

DynamoDB is a fully managed NoSQL database service provided by Amazon Web Services (AWS) that delivers fast and predictable performance at any scale. Like every database service, DynamoDB's performance and efficiency are contingent on the proper configuration of its various components. A key aspect of this configuration is understanding and managing hot keys, a common issue faced in high-volume, high-velocity data operations.

Before diving into hot key troubleshooting, it is important to firmly grasp the core concepts of DynamoDB, which can be broadly compartmentalized into tables, items, and attributes. A "table" is a collection of "items," and an "item" is composed of one or more "attributes." Depending on the use case, several access patterns may be involved, such as fetching an item, writing an item, or updating an item. Undoubtedly, efficient reading and writing operations are dependent on successful data modeling.

2.1. Data Modeling and Primary Key Selection

The selection of primary keys in DynamoDB is critical, as they uniquely identify each item in the table and support efficient access to the desired data. Primary keys include a partition key and an optional sort key. DynamoDB distributes data across multiple partitions based on the partition key, ensuring scalability and performance. The partition key's uniqueness warrants diverse and evenly spread out keys to avoid data imbalance in partitions. This is where hot keys come into play.

A "hot key" is a key that is disproportionately read or written compared to other keys. This induces undue pressure on a particular database partition, leading to skewed performance and throttling. Excessive read or write requests to a specific key can be detrimental to the overall performance of DynamoDB operations. Identifying and addressing hot key issues are essential to running cost-effective and efficient DynamoDB operations.

2.2. Recognizing Hot Key Problems

Hot key problems typically emerge under high traffic loads or because of certain dominant access patterns. For example, if many write operations are directed towards a common key, it can result in a hot key situation.

Notably, the first sign of a hot key problem could be API throttling. DynamoDB limits the total read and write activity per second for a given partition, leading to throttling when the consumed units exceed the assigned provisioned throughput. CloudWatch, AWS's monitoring service, can provide insight into throttling metrics. Here, looking at "ThrottledRequests" and "ConsumedWriteCapacityUnits" or "ConsumedReadCapacityUnits" can give a better understanding of whether there's disproportionate load on any specific partition key.

2.3. Mitigating Hot Key Issues

There are several strategies for mitigating hot key problems, each with its own strengths and constraints. The strategies are broadly based on three frameworks: access pattern adjustments, data distribution modifications, and DynamoDB feature utilization.

1. Access Pattern Adjustments: This involves changing how your application interacts with DynamoDB. Time-based batching or adopting eventual consistency for read operations can attenuate hot key issues.

2. Data Distribution Modifications: These include creating

additional fake primary keys (known as "sharding") to distribute writes and reads across multiple partition keys and consequently, across multiple partitions.

3. DynamoDB Feature Utilization: DynamoDB offers a few features that could potentially alleviate hotkey issues. Using DAX (DynamoDB Accelerator) could provide a caching layer to handle read-intensive applications, thus reducing the load on hot keys.

Through a judicious understanding of DynamoDB's primary key selection, data modeling, and efficient use of AWS monitoring tools like CloudWatch, hot key issues can be proactively identified and tackled. The strategies mentioned above, while broad and context-dependent, provide a robust foundation to approach hot key issues.

In conclusion, despite the complexity surrounding hot keys and managing them, gaining a comprehensive understanding of underlying concepts and building efficient strategies can significantly enhance the operational efficiency of your DynamoDB tables, mitigating hot key-related problems and promoting scalable and cost-effective operations.

Chapter 3. Deciphering the Concept of Hot Partitions

Understanding the concept of hot partitions in DynamoDB is paramount to ensuring optimal performance of database operations. A "hot" partition is essentially a partition that is receiving a disproportionately high amount of read or write traffic. This can lead to throttling and can significantly impact the performance of your DynamoDB table. Fortunately, understanding what causes hot partitions and how to address them can put you well on your way to managing and avoiding these issues effectively.

3.1. Hot Partition Cause

The primary cause of hot partitions in DynamoDB is data skew. Simply put, this refers to an uneven distribution of data and traffic across your table's partitions. When a single partition receives too many requests, either read or write, it 'heats up'.

When you're designing a table, you define a primary key, which is composed of a partition key and an optional sort key. DynamoDB uses the partition key's value as input to an internal hash function that determines a partition where the item will be stored. Ideally, this algorithm should evenly spread data across multiple partitions. However, if many requests target the same partition key values, they will end up targeting the same partition, and cause it to heat up.

A common scenario that could result in a hot partition is when your application's read and write operations are disproportionately aimed at a small subset of your data.

A great example of this can be noticed during a popular online sale. Here, a small set of items (the discounted ones) will be accessed much more frequently than the others (non-discounted items), causing those partitions which hold the discounted items to heat up.

3.2. Identifying a Hot Partition

Identifying a hot partition is key to alleviating the associated problems. AWS does provide a few tools, like Amazon CloudWatch and AWS CloudTrail, which can help in identifying hot partitions.

CloudWatch allows you to monitor application and system-wide performance metrics, while CloudTrail captures all API requests for Amazon DynamoDB in your AWS account.

You should look for any sudden spikes in throttled read or write events, latencies, or event durations and then cross reference these data with your access patterns and table schema to identify hot partitions.

3.3. Strategies to Avoid Hot Partitions

Preventing hot partitions from developing in the first place involves careful planning of your data model and access patterns. Following are a few strategies that can be adopted:

1. **Uniform Data Distribution**: As uneven distribution of data often leads to hot keys, it becomes essential to ensure your data is evenly distributed across partitions.

2. **Use Calculated Keys**: You can create partition keys from multiple attributes to create a larger number of unique keys, ensuring more uniform distribution of data.

3. **Key Salting**: In cases where read and write traffic can't be evenly distributed, introduce randomness to the partition key (known as 'salting') to distribute requests more evenly.

4. **DynamoDB Adaptive Capacity**: AWS introduced adaptive capacity wherein DynamoDB automatically adapplies to your traffic patterns so that you continue to drive utilization of your table evenly.

3.4. Managing Hot Partitions

Even with careful planning, you may still find yourself dealing with a hot partition. In these scenarios, you can:

1. **Add more partitions**: By increasing the number of partitions, you spread your workload across more computation resources, lessening the chance of a hot partition.

2. **Use caching**: A caching layer, such as Amazon DynamoDB Accelerator (DAX), can help reduce read traffic to your table, easing the load on a hot partition.

3. **Change your access pattern**: Modify the way you read/write to the table, especially if your workload is primarily aimed at a small subset of your data.

In summary, despite the challenges a hot partition can bring, understanding why hot partitions occur, how to identify them, and how to manage and avoid them will allow you to work confidently and effectively with DynamoDB. Given the right knowledge and strategies, hot partitions can be prevented, managed, and even put to work in your favor.

Chapter 4. Signs and Symptoms of Hot Key Issues

Spotting a hot key issue in DynamoDB is not an everyday affair. It requires a keen eye for symptoms and a sturdy understanding of underlying system behavior. Within this chapter, we will analyze the various telltale signs that could point towards a potential hot key issue. We'll also look into the subtler aspects that often get overlooked, but may prove essential for early detection and timely troubleshooting.

4.1. The Classic Signs

Among the front line symptoms of hot keys in DynamoDB, the following stand out due to their direct impact on your application's performance.

1. **Sudden Increase in Throttled Requests**: One of the primary signs of a hot key issue is an abrupt rise in the count of throttled requests. Throttling happens when a single partition receives too many read or write requests resulting in a violation of throughput limit.

2. **Uneven Request Pattern**: Hot keys give rise to disproportionate access patterns. This means that a few keys are being bombarded with a lot of read or write requests while others are not used much.

3. **Consistent High Latency**: A persistent high latency even when the average usage is within the provisioned capacity hints at a potential hot key problem.

However, these symptoms are best internalized with an in-depth understanding of how DynamoDB manages data.

4.2. Understanding How DynamoDB Stores Data

DynamoDB utilizes multiple partitions to store data and handle requests. Each of these partitions has a designated capacity, which, if exceeded, results in throttling. For instance, if your table's provisioned throughput is 5,000 read capacity units (RCUs) and 1,000 write capacity units (WCUs), and you have five partitions, each partition would handle around 1,000 RCUs and 200 WCUs. Consequently, if you have a hot key in a given partition that consumes 3,000 RCUs, it exceeds the partition's throughput limit, resulting in throttled requests.

4.3. Getting Deeper: CloudWatch Metrics and DAX Hit Rate

To arm yourself with stronger proficiency in detecting hot keys, leverage Amazon's CloudWatch. Key metrics provide valuable insights, predominantly the `ThrottledRequests` metric that indicates whether you're facing a general throughput issue or a hot key issue.

If you notice the `ProvisionedReadCapacityUnits` or `ProvisionedWriteCapacityUnits` always being low while the `ThrottledRequests` stays high, it indicates a low request diversity – a typical sign of hot keys.

A similar conclusion can be reached by utilizing the DynamoDB Accelerator (DAX) hit rate. A consistently low hit rate might hint at a specific item or a small set of items being constantly accessed, signifying a hot key situation.

4.4. Subtle Indicators: Skewed Access Pattern and Unused Capacity

Sometimes the signs aren't as palpable. More subtle indications can manifest in the form of skewed access patterns or unused provisioned capacity.

A skewed access pattern is detectable through AWS DMS. If a few items are repeatedly being read or written to, it suggests a hot key. Similarly, if you observe a large amount of unused capacity in your CloudWatch metrics, it perhaps means only a few keys are being overly accessed while the others are not - again suggesting a hot key.

4.5. The Final Clue: Sudden Surges in Latency

Unexplained spikes in latency can also be a red flag. If you're hitting high read or write latencies while your provisioned capacity is well within the limits, it might be due to hot keys causing throttling of requests.

Understanding these signs and symptoms are key to preemptive detection of hot keys, enabling you to avoid throttling, ensuring smooth operation, and ultimately leading to better usage of your provisioned throughput.

Remember, hot keys can be a significant drain on your resources and operational efficiency if not identified and rectified in a timely manner. Be proactive in continuously monitoring these signs for a more effective and reliable DynamoDB operation.

Chapter 5. Hot Key Impact on Applications and Performance

Amazon DynamoDB, a scalable NoSQL database, is lauded for its efficiency and performance capabilities, making it a popular choice for managing high-speed transactions and large workloads. However, a common challenge arises with Hot Keys, an issue that can potentially impact application performance and operational efficiency. This chapter offers a comprehensive investigation into the influence of Hot Keys on applications and performance, providing guidance and strategies to successfully navigate these challenges.

5.1. Understanding Hot Keys

To comprehend hot key impact, it's essential to first understand what a hot key is. A hot key in DynamoDB is a single partition key that is excessively read or written to, leading to request throttling despite the remaining capacity in other partitions. If multiple applications or threads make concurrent read or write calls using the same partition key, request rate can exceed capacity units allocated to that key, leading to a bottleneck known as a 'hot key'.

A detailed examination of your workload can help determine if hot key problems exist. Monitor your application's performance using Amazon CloudWatch metrics such as ThrottledRequests to identify request spikes.

5.2. Hot Key Impact on Performance

Hot keys can impact the service's ability to spread the workload evenly across partitions, causing potential performance degradation.

Excessive traffic to a single partition key can cause write and read operation latency to spike, disrupting normal functioning. Extended latencies could lead to ThrottledRequests, which, in worst-case scenarios, could result in application timeouts or failures.

It is important to analyze 'ThrottledRequests', 'ReadThrottleEvents', and 'WriteThrottleEvents' in CloudWatch to monitor request throttling situations. All these can serve as indicators of a possible hot key situation, thus highlighting the need for optimization.

5.3. Impact on Application Architecture

Hot keys not only affect performance, but also influence the design and architecture of your application. If the architecture doesn't account for hot key usage, issues such as request throttling and uneven data distribution can obstruct application functionality.

Respecting the key principles of DynamoDB architecture, such as choosing the right partition key to avoid hot keys and leveraging secondary indexes, is crucial to achieving optimum performance.

5.4. Troubleshooting Hot Keys

Identifying signs of hot keys early is vital to mitigate their impact. CloudWatch metrics are an effective tool for detecting hot keys. However, diagnosing can often be complex due to nature of distributed architectures.

To solve hot key issues, begin by analyzing your write patterns. Identifying spikes in ThrottledRequests and latency metrics related to specific partition keys can bring you a step closer to resolution.

Efficient usage of AWS's auto scaling feature can also play a significant role in management. Though not a perfect remedy as it does not solve the underlying issue, it can provide necessary breathing room before a strategic fix is implemented.

5.5. Mitigation Strategies

Once a hot key is identified, you need to implement mitigation strategies to alleviate its impact. Consider techniques such as pre-splitting partitions or introducing randomness into key selection to distribute requests more evenly across partitions.

DynamoDB DAX (DynamoDB Accelerator) is another useful strategy, reducing database read latency times by caching frequent accessed data, thereby mitigating hot keys. Employing DAX is especially helpful in read-heavy applications where hot keys are common.

In a write-intensive environment, consider employing Kinesis Data Streams for write sharding. This can alleviate write request intensity on a single partition key.

5.6. Conclusion

Hot keys can significantly impact the performance and architecture of applications using DynamoDB. Understanding their nature, identifying potential signs, and applying effective mitigation strategies are crucial for maintaining operational efficiency. Invest in comprehensive analysis of your workload, leverage DynamoDB features smartly, and consider all available AWS tools to prevent or deal with hot keys effectively. The keys to troubleshooting are vigilance, analysis, and timely action.

Chapter 6. Efficient Data Modeling to Avoid Hot Key Problems

If the keys are unevenly distributed, an issue commonly referred to as a "hot key" emerges, creating potential bottlenecks that can significantly halt the speed and effectiveness of your DynamoDB operations. Efficient data modeling plays a pivotal role in preventing such issues from arising. Let's delve into how this can be done.

The first step towards efficient data modeling is understanding your access patterns. Recalling that DynamoDB is a NoSQL database, it's vital to recognize that it caters to a different set of principles compared to traditional SQL databases. DynamoDB is designed around the premise that you know your access patterns ahead of time and model your data to accommodate these patterns accordingly.

6.1. Understanding Access Patterns

Begin by meticulously studying your application's requirements, traffic patterns, and the kind of data interactions that will be most frequent. Ask yourself critical questions such as:

- What kind of data will your application be reading and writing?

- What is the average size of each item?

- Are there patterns in terms of the frequency or timing of data accesses?

- What is the nature and frequency of write operations compared to reads?

- Will data be accessed in groups?

It's noteworthy that a well-designed DynamoDB table is typically centered around one or two main access patterns, with others being secondary.

6.2. Key Choice and Distribution

The keys you choose to utilize in your DynamoDB table hold significant importance. Keys in DynamoDB are designated into two types: Partition keys and Sort keys.

A **Partition Key** (PK), also known as a hash key, is the primary way DynamoDB organizes data. DynamoDB uses the value of the PK to distribute data across multiple partitions for scalability and performance.

A **Sort Key** (SK), also known as a range key, is used alongside a PK to provide a second level of data organization. Having a thoughtful choice of SK based around your access patterns can substantially improve your DynamoDB experience.

Selecting a PK that evenly distributes read/write operations will help avoid hot key bottlenecks. This can be achieved by ensuring the partition key has a large number of distinct values and that requests are evenly distributed across these values.

6.3. Proper Use of Secondary Indexes

Secondary indexes allow for querying data on non-key attributes or even alternate keys. They can be substantial in diversifying your access patterns and consequently, in reducing the possibility of hot key problems.

There are two type of secondary indexes in DynamoDB:

- **Global secondary index (GSI)**: An index with a hash and range key that can be different from the table's keys.

- **Local secondary index (LSI)**: An index that has the same hash key as the table, but a different range key.

Implementing secondary indexes should be done cautiously, considering your application's requirements and the provisioned read/write capacity.

6.4. Considerations for Write Sharding

If a significant portion of your data traffic tends to zero in on a small number of partition keys, consider applying write sharding. With write sharding, you add a random prefix or suffix to your partition key values to distribute the writes across multiple partitions.

For example, if you have a 'Product' partition key which has high write traffic, by appending a suffix between 1 to N (where N is a number based on desired level of distribution), you create multiple new partition keys - Product1, Product2, and so on, effectively dispersing your requests across multiple keys.

6.5. Leveraging DynamoDB Streams and AWS Lambda

Consider incorporating DynamoDB Streams and AWS Lambda. DynamoDB Streams capture table activity, and their integrated AWS Lambda triggers offer a seamless avenue to react to data modification. This setup might help in spreading out your workload, thereby reducing the chances of hot key issues.

6.6. Cost-Benefit Analysis

The cost of preventing hot key problems is, in most cases, far less than the cost of troubleshooting already occurred issues. Therefore, consider the cost-benefits of early architecture decisions regarding key schema, secondary index use, and write sharding.

In conclusion, efficient data modeling in DynamoDB involves understanding your access patterns, careful key selection and distribution, prudent use of secondary indexes, potential write sharding, leveraging DynamoDB Streams with AWS Lambda, and constant cost-benefit evaluation. All these steps, when diligently implemented, can significantly aid in avoiding and managing hot key problems.

Chapter 7. Best Practices for Key Distribution

Best practices for key distribution strategy are pivotal in optimizing DynamoDB usage, thereby mitigating the impact of hot keys. This chapter provides detailed insights using Amazon DynamoDB design models, exemplifying optimal partition key selections, offering in-depth understanding for designing a successful DynamoDB schema to eliminate hot key issues.

7.1. Identifying the Suitable Key Type

Understanding and opting for optimal key types paves the way for efficient performance. DynamoDB tables fundamentally incorporate two principal types: the partition key and the partition and sort key combination.

A solo partition key, also known as the hash key, holds a unique attribute identity. DynamoDB employs an internal hash function on this key to determine the partition that should house the respective item. Simultaneously, the hash values evenly distribute across all available partitions.

The partition and sort key combination, in contrast, works differently. The partition key behaves just like in the previous instance; however, this combination introduces an additional sort key. Within any partition, the items with the same partition key get sorted based on this sort key, thereby adding an extra layer of organization within individual partitions.

7.2. Primary Key Design: Avoiding Hot Partitions

The partition key becomes crucial due to its direct link to partition usability. The primary consideration should be to enable even distribution of data and access patterns across partitions. Overloading a single partition by excessively reading or writing harms performance due to throttling, recapitulating the hot key issue.

A well-distributed key design ensures equal workload allocation among various partitions, averting potential hot partition situations. For instance, choosing an attribute with high-cardinality values such as UserId or unique OrderId fosters even data distribution, as long as the access pattern remains predictable and uniform.

Here are some strategies to optimize your primary key design:

1. Tie the partition key to high-cardinality attributes ensuring substantial unique values.

2. Avoid using attributes with low-cardinality, like item type or status, as these could lead to unbalanced data dispersion.

3. Confirm that the access pattern is distributed across multiple partition keys.

7.3. Using Partitions Efficiently

For DynamoDB tables with heavy write demands, using partitions efficiently becomes critical. Spreading your data across multiple partition keys ensures good write performance.

Remember, DynamoDB designates throughput depending on your provisioned capacity units per partition. For instance, if a table's write capacity is set to 3000 Write Capacity Units (WCU) and

DynamoDB provides three partitions, each partition receives 1000 WCUs. Hence, intensely focusing the write operation on one partition key will not benefit from the total WCUs.

Here are some suggestions for effectively using partitions:

1. Have a random suffix or prefix to the partition key value. It helps to spread write operations uniformly across multiple partitions.

2. Implement sharding. It involves creating artificial partition key values to spread traffic across multiple partitions.

3. Use the 'DynamoDB Adaptive Capacity' feature to temporarily sustain imbalance between partitions.

7.4. Leverage Secondary Indexes

Secondary indexes provide alternate data access patterns. A secondary index encapsulates a subset of attributes from the table, with an alternate key to support query operations. While secondary indexes are great tools to optimize read operations, an unplanned index might lead to extra charges, wasted resources, and potential hot keys.

It's advisable to follow these practices:

1. Only create secondary indexes that truly enhance your access patterns.

2. Monitor the indexes for usage and remove underutilized indexes.

3. Use sparse indexes responsibly, where items only get indexed when they possess certain attributes.

4. Remember, excessively writing to indexes might also lead to hot key situations.

7.5. Reviewing and Adapting Your Strategy

Lastly, never consider your key distribution strategy as a 'set-and-forget' plan. Always monitor your application's behavior and adapt your strategy considering factors such as access patterns, data growth, DynamoDB updates, and application requirements.

Consider these steps for reviewing your strategy:

1. Monitor your DynamoDB metrics and CloudWatch alarms to identify any surges related to throttling or hot keys.

2. Learn from your usage patterns and continue refining your partition, sort key usage, and index efficiency.

3. Make use of AWS DMS (Database Migration Service) for changing the database schema without downtime.

Through detailed understanding and effective implementation of these key distribution best practices, you can assure the operational efficiency of your DynamoDB, mitigating chances of incurring hot keys. Embrace the guidance above and continually evolve your strategy – therein lies the best chance at harnessing the full potential of DynamoDB.

Chapter 8. Mitigating Hot Key Issues in Large-Scale Applications

Effective management of Hot Key issues is critical for the seamless operation of large-scale applications. This discourse dives into detailed strategies and measures you can take to efficiently mitigate these concerns.

8.1. Understanding the Hot Key Phenomenon

Before tackling the solution, we need a clear understanding of the problem at hand. A hot key in the context of DynamoDB is a partition key value that is overwhelmed with read or write traffic. This uneven distribution of data access can cause throttling issues leading to ineffective resource utilization.

8.2. Identifying Hot Keys

The first step towards addressing hot key issues involves identifying them. AWS provides several tools which can help spot these anomalies, like AWS CloudWatch. By tracking the `ConsumedReadCapacityUnits` and `ConsumedWriteCapacityUnits`, one can ascertain if a specific partition key is getting an unusual amount of traffic.

8.3. Practice Data Distributing

One of the fundamental practices in mitigating hot keys is proper data distributing. Spreading your data across multiple partition keys rather than a single one, aids in avoiding hot keys. DynamoDB automatically distributes data across partitions for easy, quick, and efficient access.

Another effective approach is the use of "salting" your partition keys by appending or prepending a random value. This ensures data is uniformly distributed across several partitions.

8.4. Implement Write Sharding

Write sharding is a technique where multiple write target items are used in scenarios where you know the write load is likely to exceed the throughput of a single partition. This helps in uniformly spreading the load, thus avoiding any single hot partition key.

8.5. Adopting Adaptive Capacity

DynamoDB's adaptive capacity feature is a boon when dealing with hot keys. This feature allows your application to continue read and write operations on hot partitions without being throttled, even if the traffic exceeds the provisioned throughput.

8.6. Using DAX (DynamoDB Accelerator)

DAX is a fully managed, highly available in-memory cache that can offload read traffic from your tables to reduce latency and increase throughput. While it doesn't directly solve the hot key problem, it reduces read load on hot keys which helps alleviate the issue.

8.7. Retrospective Review

Performing retrospective reviews on how hot keys are generated and analysing specific usage patterns can betoken potential issues. Adopting preventive measures based on these insights can help minimize the impact of hot key issue.

8.8. Automated Throttling Alerts

Calcitrant hot keys can become a major bottleneck for the application's performance. Consider setting up automated throttling alerts. These alerts will notify you when the throttling thresholds are breached enabling immediate action.

8.9. Leverage Utilities

In critical situations, certain utilities like Amazon EMR or AWS Glue can be instrumental in migrating large amounts of data between tables or changing the schema of an existing one, thus mitigating potential hot key issues.

Managing hot key issues in large-scale applications is a blend of reactive and proactive approaches. With these insights, you are now well-equipped to not only address hot key issues effectively but also enhance your application's performance and reliability. Remember, understanding the problem before seeking solutions forms the fulcrum of this endeavour.

Chapter 9. Detailed Walk-Through of Hot Key Troubleshooting

DynamoDB, with its highly distributed architecture, offers a robust platform to support high-performance workloads. But like any technology, it has its challenges – one of them being hot keys. Toppling the balance in work distribution, hot keys can often lead to throttling and can essentially slow down operations. Thus, understanding what hot keys are, how they form, why they're problematic, and crucially, how to troubleshoot them, is indispensable.

9.1. Defining Hot Keys

Simply put, a hot key is a partition key that is written to excessively, leading to an imbalance in work distribution. DynamoDB operates on the fundamental idea of 'Partition Key' – every item that you store in your DynamoDB is uniquely identifiable by its partition key. With every write request, DynamoDB writes data to a node (physical storage area), determined by the partition key. Hence, if one partition key is written to extensively it could lead to potential bottlenecks, colloquially referred to as 'hot keys'.

9.2. How Hot Keys Form

Hot keys are an unfortunate consequence of uneven data access patterns. For illustration, suppose you're running an eCommerce store with hundreds of products. Product #123 is a hot-selling item that receives substantially more hits than other products. Over time, the partition key associated with Product #123 becomes a hot key due to heavy write and read operations.

The formation of hot keys is further aggravated when a single partition has to handle more read and write traffic than it can manage. Its capacity to work is defined by the number of Read Capacity Units (RCUs) and Write Capacity Units (WCUs). Faced with incoming traffic beyond these capacity units, operations get throttled.

9.3. The Perils of Hot Keys

An uneven work distribution strain, as with hot keys, leads to inefficient use of resources and throttling. Given DynamoDB's pricing model, where costs are directly tied to RCUs and WCUs, hot keys have the potential to dramatically inflate costs, while reducing efficiency – a harmful combo no operation desires.

9.4. Detecting Hot Keys

The first step for troubleshooting is detection. For hot keys, AWS CloudWatch can be employed to monitor your DynamoDB's performance. You can customize your CloudWatch dashboard to track metrics like ConsumedReadCapacityUnits and ConsumedWriteCapacityUnits for individual tables and global secondary indexes (GSIs).

Make a note to particularly observe the `ProvisionedThroughputExceeded` system errors – this might be an alarm bell for possible hot keys. Also, if there is an increase in `ConsumedRCUs` or `ConsumedWCUs` even without a proportionate increase in traffic, it's another hint at the incidence of hot keys.

9.5. Addressing Hot Keys

Once you've detected potential hot keys, the next step is mitigation. Here are ways to troubleshoot this problem:

1+| ===

|**Solution** |**Method** |1. Sharding| Employ sharding to distribute traffic more evenly. Sharding transforms the partition key by applying techniques like salting, random suffix or prefix, to further distribute your data. |2. GSIs | Use GSIs to evenly distribute data without disrupting table layout. |3. Adjust Capacity| Review and adjust your capacity units to accommodate increased traffic. |4. Optimise Code | Review your code and access patterns to ensure they're not leading to hot keys. |5. Use DynamoDB Accelerator | Use DynamoDB Accelerator (DAX) to mitigate hot keys by caching responses to repeated requests. ===

Each of these requires careful planning along with regular review and adjustment. Trust me, tackling hot keys is no cakewalk. However, prevention is often more straightforward than a cure.

9.6. Preventing Hot Keys

Preventing the formation of hot keys is possible with thoughtful planning of your write and read strategies. Sharding, as mentioned, can be a fantastic preventative measure – if you apply salting, random suffixing, etc., to your partition key right off the bat, you distribute those writes more evenly, preventing any single partition from handling too much.

Consider a time-based approach, especially relevant for time-series data, where the partition key changes over time, thereby avoiding repeated hits on the same partition.

Additionally, understanding your access patterns is crucial. DynamoDB is a fantastic service that can manage enormous workloads with optimal efficiency if used correctly. But misuse, especially via misuse of the partition key, can lead to complications such as hot keys.

In conclusion, understanding and managing hot keys is invaluable for any DynamoDB operator. By being proactive, analysing performance metrics, optimising your access patterns, and refining capacity units, you can ensure your operations run smoothly and efficiently. Like any other aspect of working with DynamoDB, it's an iterative process and will require regular attention and adjustment. But, armed with this knowledge, you're well-equipped to tackle hot keys and the challenges they present.

Chapter 10. Advanced Techniques for Hot Key Resolution

Diving right in, hot keys in DynamoDB pose one of the most complex challenges that developers and administrators face. Often a result of an unbalanced workload distribution across partitions, hot keys can lead to uneven resource usage, resulting in bottlenecks and hampering the desired high performance of your DynamoDB operations. Let's take a detailed look into this issue and explore advanced techniques for hot key resolution.

10.1. Understanding Hot Keys In-Depth

Before we progress towards the solution, we need to understand the anatomy of our problem. A hot key is essentially an item or attribute that is excessively read/written, causing too many requests to a single partition. Such excessively accessed keys can have substantial impact on the application's performance, often leading to increased response times and throttling.

Despite automated traffic partitioning, uniquely identifying items can still fail to provide an evenly distributed access pattern. In such cases, disproportionately high traffic may be directed towards a few keys, making them hot. As DynamoDB operates on a provisioned throughput model, an excessive load on a few keys can easily exceed the provisioned capacity of these partitions.

10.2. Diagnosing Hot Keys

Before you can resolve a problem, you need to diagnose it. Amazon CloudWatch can be particularly useful for detecting hot keys. By monitoring and analyzing 'ReadThrottleEvents' or 'WriteThrottleEvents', you can gauge if your application is trying to access a hot key excessively.

Moreover, AWS DynamoDB's 'ConsumedReadCapacityUnits' or 'ConsumedWriteCapacityUnits' can furnish valuable insights about your traffic pattern, thus aiding in hot key detection.

10.3. Utilizing Adaptive Capacity

One of the advanced techniques to solve hot key problems is Adaptive Capacity. Introduced by DynamoDB, Adaptive Capacity offers an automated solution to uneven workloads by adjusting capacity on-the-fly for throttled partitions. It automatically identifies partitions requiring more resources, increasing their capacity to match the demand.

Employing Adaptive Capacity can hence resolve throttling issues in minutes, providing a robust buffer against initial design errors and traffic predictions.

10.4. Implementing Data Distribution Strategies

Another essential measure to tackle hot key issues is an effective data distribution strategy.

DynamoDB's partition key design plays an instrumental role in data distribution across partitions. A monotonically increasing or decreasing partition key, or a heavily accessed key can potentially lead to hot keys. To circumvent this, introduce randomness or add a hash function to the partition key.

Distributing read/write operations randomly over a set of logical partition keys can further help in evenly distributing the load. By following such prudent design choices, you can avert hot key related problems from the outset.

10.5. Using DAX (DynamoDB Accelerator)

Leveraging DAX can be another powerful tool for resolving hot key related issues. A fully managed, highly available, in-memory cache for DynamoDB, DAX can accelerate read operations by up to 10 times, even at millions of requests per second. By reducing read traffic to the DynamoDB table, it indirectly aids in addressing the hot key issue.

Before seeing DAX as a one-stop solution, though, bear in mind the trade-offs. This technique primarily improves read-intensive workloads, thus may not be as effective with write-intensive ones. Moreover, integration with DAX involves additional costs and minor code changes.

10.6. Applying Exponential Backoff Strategy

Last but not least, the Exponential Backoff Strategy is a powerful technique to handle hot keys. In the face of 'ProvisionedThroughputExceededException', this strategy progressively increases wait times between successive retry attempts, providing much-needed relief to the overwhelmed partition.

Remember, this strategy is not a solution to the core problem but rather a short-term remediation to avoid cascading failures while the main issue is being addressed.

By employing these advanced techniques, we can effectively mitigate the challenges that hot keys present in DynamoDB. However, remember that each situation is unique. Every solution comes with its pros and cons, making tailored approaches necessary for different scenarios. Understanding the root cause and selecting the appropriate strategies are instrumental for successfully troubleshooting hot key issues in your DynamoDB operations.

Chapter 11. Maintaining Hot Key Health: Tools, Metrics and Monitoring Techniques

Hot key health checks are vital in maintaining balance in the DynamoDB setup. These checks alllow administrators to maintain optimal performance and avoid bottlenecks that can result from hot key issues. In this chapter, we delve into the various tools, metrics, and monitoring techniques that help in maintaining and improving hot key health.

Comprehending the health of hot keys comprises three main facets - identifying the hot keys, assessing their health, and remediation.

11.1. Identifying Hot Keys

To maintain the health of hot keys, we must first identify them. A hot key is any key that receives more traffic than other keys in your table. By keeping tabs on the read and write traffic of each key, we can identify potential hot keys.

Amazon CloudWatch is a vital tool for this task. It provides metrics that you can monitor to keep an eye on the usage of each of your table keys. Focus on two major metrics:

- `ProvisionedReadCapacityUnits`: This metric gives you an idea of the read traffic each key is handling.

- `ProvisionedWriteCapacityUnits`: It shows you the write traffic of each key.

Monitoring these metrics allows you to identify potential hot keys and address them before they negatively impact your table's performance.

11.2. Health Assessment of Hot Keys

Once you have identified potential hot keys, the next step is assessing their health. The health of a key is determined by comparing its current usage to your estimated usage.

You can use AWS DynamoDB's built-in mechanisms to get an overview of your key usage. For example, DynamoDB Adaptive Capacity is an automatic management feature that evenly spreads your workload across your table's partitions. If you see a sharp increase in usage on one partition, this could be indicative of a hot key issue.

11.3. Remediation

Understanding how to remediate a hot key depends on the nature of your application. If your application uses hot keys due to its design, you might need to rethink your key model, partition-key choice, or even distribute your requests more evenly.

In case of unexpected spikes in usage, consider implementing a backoff and retry strategy. It will help you avoid request throttling and maintain a consistent performance in your application.

For instance, DynamoDB's Auto Scaling feature can automatically manage throughputs to maintain performance during an increase in demand.

11.4. Employing Tools and Monitoring Techniques

Choosing the appropriate tools and monitoring techniques is a significant step towards maintaining hot key health. Comprehensive monitoring can help identify potential problems before they cascade into bigger issues.

- AWS CloudWatch Alarms: These can be set on the DynamoDB metrics to notify you when certain thresholds are breached, helping you take action promptly.

- AWS DAX (DynamoDB Accelerator): This in-memory cache can assist in reducing the load on your main table, thus preventing your hot keys from becoming overburdened.

- Amazon DynamoDB Streams: This service records all changes (Insert/Update/Delete) made in the DynamoDB table. It can be coupled with AWS Lambda to take corrective action based on the nature of database changes occurring in quick successions at short intervals.

- AWS Trusted Advisor: This provides automated checks on resources provisioned in AWS accounts, advising if the resources are approaching thresholds or if there's a possibility of a hot key.

11.5. Metrics to Monitor

Monitoring key metrics can greatly aid in managing hot key health. Below are some of the crucial metrics to keep tabs on:

- ReadCapacityUnits and WriteCapacityUnits: These provide insight into the amount of read and write activity on a particular key.

- ConsumedReadCapacityUnits and ConsumedWriteCapacityUnits: They indicate the capacity consumed by your application and are signs of potential hot key problems if the values are consistently high.

- ThrottledRequests: If there are a large number of throttled requests, this might be a sign of potential hot key issues.

- SystemErrors: These errors usually point to issues with your DynamoDB setup.

In conclusion, maintaining the health of hot keys in DynamoDB involves the correct identification of hot keys, the regular assessment of their health, implementing right remediation measures, and the consistent monitoring of vital metrics. By following these methods, you can preemptively tackle hot key-related problems, thereby ensuring the seamless operation of your DynamoDB.

By regularly utilizing tools, monitoring techniques, and understanding the key metrics in DynamoDB, you can uphold the operational efficiency of your setup. This, combined with a good grasp of troubleshooting methods, will help you master hot key management in any DynamoDB scenario.